DON'T SWEAT
THE SMALL STUFF
FOR WOMEN
JOURNAL

DON'T SWEAT
THE SMALL STUFF
FOR WOMEN
JOURNAL

KRISTINE CARLSON

HYPERION

New York

ISBN: 0-7868-8766-4

Hyperion books are available for special promotions and premiums.
For details contact Hyperion Special Markets, 77 West 66th Street,
11th floor, New York, New York, 10023, or call 212-456-0100.

FIRST EDITION

10 9 8 7 6 5 4 3 2 1

DON'T SWEAT
THE SMALL STUFF
FOR WOMEN
JOURNAL

You don't have to do it all—it's okay to shed your "Wonder Woman" image and ask for help when you need it.

_____

_____

_____

_____

_____

_____

_____

_____

_____

_____

_____

_____

_____

_____

Choose to start each day with an inspirational thought, a clear mind, and a smile. A peaceful morning ritual makes an enormous difference in everyday living.

_____

_____

_____

_____

_____

_____

_____

_____

_____

_____

_____

_____

_____

Volunteer your time, but choose what you truly enjoy so that you don't become over-committee-d.

_____

_____

_____

_____

_____

_____

_____

_____

_____

_____

_____

_____

_____

_____

_____

Love, cherish, and appreciate your friends just the way they are.

_____

_____

_____

_____

_____

_____

_____

_____

_____

_____

_____

_____

_____

_____

Feel peace in knowing that, in this moment, life is great.

_____

_____

_____

_____

_____

_____

_____

_____

_____

_____

_____

_____

_____

_____

Celebrate your own uniqueness as a woman. Your beauty comes from feeling good about yourself from the inside.

_____

_____

_____

_____

_____

_____

_____

_____

_____

_____

_____

_____

_____

_____

Listening to someone that you care for is a simple way to show you care. It says to them: "I'm here for you."

Much of life is made up of mundane, "small-stuff" tasks. Clear your path for the day, and meditate. Find some comfort in doing the ordinary.

Enjoy yourself in nature, and nurture your spirit by going outdoors and getting "down and dirty" with a little dirt now and then.

_____

_____

_____

_____

_____

_____

_____

_____

_____

_____

_____

_____

_____

Don't dwell on what you should have, would have, or could have done. Learn from the past, focus on the present moment, and deal with things the way that they are.

_____

_____

_____

_____

_____

_____

_____

_____

_____

_____

_____

_____

_____

_____

Resist the urge to stir emotional pots. Save pot-stirring for dinner, and avoid unnecessary angst and stress.

Speak to your loved ones from a calm and loving place in your heart. Especially if you're angry, speak from your love.

_____

_____

_____

_____

_____

_____

_____

_____

_____

_____

_____

_____

_____

Your love is located in your heart. When in conflict, listen from your heart—and your love—and set your ego aside.

_____

_____

_____

_____

_____

_____

_____

_____

_____

_____

_____

_____

_____

It's easy to see faults in others, but it takes courage and insight to look in the mirror and see your own flaws. Remember this: There is no perfect person on Earth.

_____

_____

_____

_____

_____

_____

_____

_____

_____

_____

_____

_____

_____

The adventure in life is in not always knowing what's going to happen next, so go with the twists and turns that lead to your greater life plan.

_____

_____

_____

_____

_____

_____

_____

_____

_____

_____

_____

_____

_____

Share life's little unpleasantries and stresses with your bosom buddy—make an annual date for a mammogram together.

_____

_____

_____

_____

_____

_____

_____

_____

_____

_____

_____

_____

_____

_____

Create the precious and priceless gift of memories for your children—and yourself. Loving memories of family are irreplaceable.

_____

_____

_____

_____

_____

_____

_____

_____

_____

_____

_____

_____

_____

To be reflective is to be spiritually rich. Quiet your mind, be humble, and ask your inner self for guidance.

Create your own personal stress-buster rituals to help you stop sweating the small stuff.

_____

_____

_____

_____

_____

_____

_____

_____

_____

_____

_____

_____

_____

_____

_____

Don't take the behavior and actions of others personally. You'll experience less frustration if you ignore erroneous thoughts and feelings.

_____

_____

_____

_____

_____

_____

_____

_____

_____

_____

_____

_____

_____

Draft your family to help around the house. Everyone is happier when they contribute to the family's well-being.

_____

_____

_____

_____

_____

_____

_____

_____

_____

_____

_____

_____

_____

_____

Be truly happy for the successes of others. You don't need to keep up with the Joneses.

_____

_____

_____

_____

_____

_____

_____

_____

_____

_____

_____

_____

_____

_____

Each of us has a unique set of gifts and talents. Find your gifts, and then follow your heart and share them freely with others.

_____

_____

_____

_____

_____

_____

_____

_____

_____

_____

_____

_____

_____

_____

_____

Nourish your spirit by taking time to reflect and rejuvenate each day. You'll find your peaceful center and see what's important in your life.

_____

_____

_____

_____

_____

_____

_____

_____

_____

_____

_____

_____

_____

Stop sweeping your frustrations under the rug! Let your steam out lightly by speaking what's on your mind—*when* it's on your mind—in a gentle way.

_____

_____

_____

_____

_____

_____

_____

_____

_____

_____

_____

_____

_____

Accept compliments with "thank you." To accept gracefully, with gratitude, is to invite divine energy directly to us.

_____

_____

_____

_____

_____

_____

_____

_____

_____

_____

_____

_____

_____

Don't send e-mail in the heat of the moment. Cool off and think before you hit the "send" button.

_____

_____

_____

_____

_____

_____

_____

_____

_____

_____

_____

_____

_____

Your sense of well-being is your own special light of peace that you carry inside you.

Learn to recognize the difference between intuition and fear. Make important decisions from a place of strength.

_____

_____

_____

_____

_____

_____

_____

_____

_____

_____

_____

_____

_____

_____

Don't let others take advantage of you. Learn to set clear boundaries and reduce the stress in your life that comes from resentment.

_____

_____

_____

_____

_____

_____

_____

_____

_____

_____

_____

_____

_____

Life rarely turns out exactly as you've planned. Let go of too-high expectations and enjoy what life brings you.

_____

_____

_____

_____

_____

_____

_____

_____

_____

_____

_____

_____

_____

A little self-doubt is healthy, but don't let too much self-doubt keep you from accomplishing your goals.

Your ability to forgive reflects the measure of love that you give yourself and others.

Skip shallow, superficial communications and instead "be real" with others. Open up, be honest, and speak from your heart.

_____

_____

_____

_____

_____

_____

_____

_____

_____

_____

_____

_____

_____

_____

Don't let PMS get the best of you. Handle yourself with care, and let others know what's going on in your life.

_____

_____

_____

_____

_____

_____

_____

_____

_____

_____

_____

_____

_____

_____

"Love" doesn't mean having a high stress limit. You'll thrive when you lower your threshold to stress and learn true patience.

Your children learn from your actions, but they won't become exactly like you. Appreciate the ways in which they grow into their own shoes.

_____

_____

_____

_____

_____

_____

_____

_____

_____

_____

_____

_____

Write a heartfelt letter to a loved one, reflect on what you've written, and use what you learn to make your relationship better. (If you want to, mail the letter!)

_____

_____

_____

_____

_____

_____

_____

_____

_____

_____

_____

_____

_____

_____

As you gather new material things, let go of old ones.

_____

_____

_____

_____

_____

_____

_____

_____

_____

_____

_____

_____

_____

_____

Don't swim upstream and fight battles that you can't win—change your attitude instead, so that you can coast downstream with ease.

_____

_____

_____

_____

_____

_____

_____

_____

_____

_____

_____

_____

Avoid "backseat living" and let others steer their own lives. Let them know that you love them just the way they are.

Learn who you are on the inside. Cultivate your inner beauty so that you radiate peace and joy on the outside.

Create better relationships and live in harmony with others by allowing for their different points of view.

_____

_____

_____

_____

_____

_____

_____

_____

_____

_____

_____

_____

_____

Don't magnify your flaws or the flaws of others. Accept that everything is how it was meant to be.

Marvel at the miracle of your ability to give birth, and celebrate this with other women.

_____

_____

_____

_____

_____

_____

_____

_____

_____

_____

_____

_____

_____

_____

Meditate, and experience the wonderful bridge connecting your mind, body, and spirit.

_____

_____

_____

_____

_____

_____

_____

_____

_____

_____

_____

_____

_____

Get negative feelings off your chest—just once—and feel good about doing it. Then let them go.

_____

_____

_____

_____

_____

_____

_____

_____

_____

_____

_____

_____

_____

Set your own priorities and be true to them. Live life the way *you* want to live it.

_____

_____

_____

_____

_____

_____

_____

_____

_____

_____

_____

_____

_____

_____

Let go of your emotional baggage. You are remarkably strong and can handle most anything that comes your way.

_____

_____

_____

_____

_____

_____

_____

_____

_____

_____

_____

_____

_____

Pack your real baggage lightly, too—you'll have more fun on your trip, and less frustration.

_____

_____

_____

_____

_____

_____

_____

_____

_____

_____

_____

_____

_____

When you're caught on a "hamster wheel" of repeating negative thoughts, simply step off. Remember that your thinking affects how you feel.

_____

_____

_____

_____

_____

_____

_____

_____

_____

_____

_____

_____

_____

Spirituality is about nourishing your own spirit, as well as nurturing others. Use your career as your spiritual work by finding everyday ways to serve.

_____

_____

_____

_____

_____

_____

_____

_____

_____

_____

_____

_____

_____

_____

Your ego keeps you from communicating with your true self. Hold your ego at bay, and soar as you connect with who you really are.

_____

_____

_____

_____

_____

_____

_____

_____

_____

_____

_____

_____

_____

We are all here to guide and learn from each other. Whether it be soul mate or soul sister, stay open to meeting new friends.

We are different—and beautiful—at every age. Find your individual path to peace of spirit, and you will truly age gracefully.

_____

_____

_____

_____

_____

_____

_____

_____

_____

_____

_____

_____

_____

_____

_____

Appreciate your partner's special, individual talents, and accept that he won't have an "eye" for everything.

_____

_____

_____

_____

_____

_____

_____

_____

_____

_____

_____

_____

_____

_____

_____

_____

Clear your head, empty your mind, and go inside yourself to learn to live in the moment.

_____

_____

_____

_____

_____

_____

_____

_____

_____

_____

_____

_____

_____

Find your unique style of dress and enjoy yourself! You'll love who you are, and you'll soar with self-confidence.

Collect physical reminders of your spiritual moments to help make the connection between your outer world and your rich inner life.

You can choose how to handle sticky situations. Remain calm, and don't sweat the small stuff.

_____

_____

_____

_____

_____

_____

_____

_____

_____

_____

_____

_____

_____

_____

_____

Don't be structure-stiff! Shift your routine to uplift your spirit, and open yourself to wonderful new possibilities.

If you're grateful for the small things in life, you'll be happy a majority of the time, and you'll find cause for celebration almost everywhere.

Find a way to honor your mother today. Write her a heartfelt note, just to give her your love and thanks.

Celebrate the life that you have. If you're single, know that life alone is cause for celebration, too.

Find your own way as you blend career and family. You are fortunate to have choices.

Share the natural good feeling that comes from inside. Enthusiasm is healthy, nourishing, and contagious.

_____

_____

_____

_____

_____

_____

_____

_____

_____

_____

_____

_____

_____

_____

Don't be afraid to build someone else up. Share positive news and nice stories about friends, family, and coworkers.

_____

_____

_____

_____

_____

_____

_____

_____

_____

_____

_____

_____

_____

_____

_____

Don't make a commitment if your heart's not in it. You can say no without feeling guilty.

Give yourself extra time between "doing" and "going." Think of this "time rebate" as time for *you*.

Treat yourself to a relaxing, nourishing retreat with your favorite girlfriends, whether it's for a weekend or just an evening. Recharge together and empower each other.

_____

_____

_____

_____

_____

_____

_____

_____

_____

_____

_____

_____

You aren't what you do—you are *you*, a person who does many things. Appreciate the richness and variety of them all.

_____

_____

_____

_____

_____

_____

_____

_____

_____

_____

_____

_____

_____

Thoughts are powerful tools. Use them to your advantage when life becomes overwhelming.

_____

_____

_____

_____

_____

_____

_____

_____

_____

_____

_____

_____

_____

_____

On those days when it seems that everything goes wrong, laugh! There really is humor in the "small stuff."

_____

_____

_____

_____

_____

_____

_____

_____

_____

_____

_____

_____

_____

_____

Leave a blank day in your daily planner, with nothing scheduled. This "inspiration flow" day is for you to live moment-to-moment and experience total freedom.

Got a gripe with someone? Talk it over with the person directly to resolve the issue and reach understanding.

_____

_____

_____

_____

_____

_____

_____

_____

_____

_____

_____

_____

_____

_____

Surprise your partner with a spontaneous sexy moment or "love attack." Reawaken your passions and have fun!

Resist the temptation to gossip about others—make your life 99 percent gossip-free.

_____

_____

_____

_____

_____

_____

_____

_____

_____

_____

_____

_____

_____

_____

A backup babysitter is insurance for a rainy day. Find one before you need one.

_____

_____

_____

_____

_____

_____

_____

_____

_____

_____

_____

_____

_____

To weigh yourself every day is an obsessive habit. Relax and focus on life, instead of your weight.

_____

_____

_____

_____

_____

_____

_____

_____

_____

_____

_____

_____

_____

_____

You are a spiritual being having a human experience. As your
material needs are met, turn to your spiritual concerns—what
really matters is how well you learn to love.

_____

_____

_____

_____

_____

_____

_____

_____

_____

_____

_____

_____

_____

Let technology work for you, not against you. Know when to hit the "off" button, and keep a healthy balance in your life.

Reacting with anger accomplishes little. Take a few deep breaths and approach problems with a level attitude.

_____

_____

_____

_____

_____

_____

_____

_____

_____

_____

_____

_____

_____

_____

You *can* take a break to recharge your spirit—seize some of the many opportunities that come your way.

_____

_____

_____

_____

_____

_____

_____

_____

_____

_____

_____

_____

_____

_____

When problems and small stuff narrow your focus, look at the big picture to open your mind and gain perspective.

Life is constantly changing. Be honest about what you need to feel nourished, and share your changing needs with others.

_____

_____

_____

_____

_____

_____

_____

_____

_____

_____

_____

_____

_____

Stay in control by fighting fires with a "controlled burn": Remain calm and collected for a more powerful, meaningful impact.

_____

_____

_____

_____

_____

_____

_____

_____

_____

_____

_____

_____

_____

_____

_____

Before adding anything to your life that you don't need, think about what it means down the road. Saying no now is preventive, and can make for a more calm and peaceful life.

Taking the advice of friends just might help solve your problems, so try saying "Hey, that's a great idea!"—and then act upon it.

Life is magical, and often pretty funny! Learn to take things less seriously and smile about what once drove you crazy.

Celebrate your femininity! Treat yourself to some luscious new lingerie, and feel blessed for being a woman.

Know your emotional hot spots well enough to see warning signs—heed them, and you'll be happier and less likely to sweat the small stuff.

_____

_____

_____

_____

_____

_____

_____

_____

_____

_____

_____

_____

_____

When a door of opportunity opens in your life, follow your heart. If you choose to walk through it, do so with faith that you're on the right path.

_____

_____

_____

_____

_____

_____

_____

_____

_____

_____

_____

_____

Your emotions are yours, whether they're happiness and joy, or sorrow and anger. You alone have the power to change them.

_____

_____

_____

_____

_____

_____

_____

_____

_____

_____

_____

_____

_____

_____

Experiment with doing nothing. A minute or two a day in quiet solitude can be magical and inspiring, and can remind you that being human is about being alive.

_____

_____

_____

_____

_____

_____

_____

_____

_____

_____

_____

_____

_____

Locate your "compassion corner" deep inside yourself, and do small things of service with great love.

_____

_____

_____

_____

_____

_____

_____

_____

_____

_____

_____

_____

_____

_____

Moods can change from moment to moment. Low moods don't last, so let them pass—then tackle your problems with a positive mood.

_____

_____

_____

_____

_____

_____

_____

_____

_____

_____

_____

_____

_____

When you climb your mountains, focus on what's in front of you and move forward one step at a time.

_____

_____

_____

_____

_____

_____

_____

_____

_____

_____

_____

_____

_____

_____

The big stuff in life is truly big—the rest is the small stuff. The more things in life that you define as small, the more you'll keep life's irritations in perspective.

Your life is full of challenges, rewards, and meaning. Look to yourself to fulfill your needs, and know that you can stand on your own two feet.

_____

_____

_____

_____

_____

_____

_____

_____

_____

_____

_____

_____

The world is at your fingertips. Spread your wings, fly like the wind, and treasure the journey of your life.

Life is ever-changing. Take time to reflect on your priorities and expectations, and make adjustments when needed.

_____

_____

_____

_____

_____

_____

_____

_____

_____

_____

_____

_____

_____

Don't let life's complexity and busy-ness stress you out. Ease into your day with a sense of peace, and you'll face it with more confidence.

_____

_____

_____

_____

_____

_____

_____

_____

_____

_____

_____

_____

_____

Contribute what you can to doing good works, but take on only what you can handle with ease.

_____

_____

_____

_____

_____

_____

_____

_____

_____

_____

_____

_____

_____

The best friends in the world are those who remember—and accept—that we're all just human.

Show your children the importance of living in the moment so that they can enjoy everyday life.

Take good care of yourself—you're as beautiful as you feel.

Be understanding and compassionate when your loved ones need
to vent problems or frustrations. Fill their need to be listened to
with compassion and understanding.

It can be easier to keep order inside of you when things are neat on the outside.

_____

_____

_____

_____

_____

_____

_____

_____

_____

_____

_____

_____

_____

_____

In every girl, there's a little bit of boy. Let go of your clean-cut self and get a bit dirty for fun! (You can always wash it off!)

_____

_____

_____

_____

_____

_____

_____

_____

_____

_____

_____

_____

_____

_____

Learn life lessons from your mistakes, and then make different choices the next time around.

_____

_____

_____

_____

_____

_____

_____

_____

_____

_____

_____

_____

_____

What you say isn't as important as the feelings that come through with your words.

When people communicate from heart to heart, a magical thing happens—they are pulled closer together.

Each person in your life can teach you something about yourself.
We are like mirrors, reflecting ourselves to each other.

_____

_____

_____

_____

_____

_____

_____

_____

_____

_____

_____

_____

_____

_____

What appears to be a negative on the surface may later turn out
to be the very stepping-stone of your success.

_____

_____

_____

_____

_____

_____

_____

_____

_____

_____

_____

_____

_____

Good buddies motivate each other to follow through on things neither of you look forward to.

Keep valued and treasured family traditions alive by passing them on to your children.

_____

_____

_____

_____

_____

_____

_____

_____

_____

_____

_____

_____

_____

_____

Open up to your inner world and embark on the greatest adventure of life: getting to know and understand yourself.

Do something physical nearly every day—it helps your mental health and clarity, too.

Break the habit of overreacting and making speedy assumptions and judgments. Step back and see the bigger picture.

Drop the "I'll do it all myself" mentality—ask for help when you need it.

_____

_____

_____

_____

_____

_____

_____

_____

_____

_____

_____

_____

_____

_____

Fears and jealousies can hold you back in life. The ability to be happy for others is a sign of mental health.

_____

_____

_____

_____

_____

_____

_____

_____

_____

_____

_____

_____

_____

Giving the gift of love—in a service-oriented way—is the most magnificent gift of all.

_____

_____

_____

_____

_____

_____

_____

_____

_____

_____

_____

_____

_____

Life is not an emergency—you can accomplish more and give more to others if you slow down and take time for yourself.

_____

_____

_____

_____

_____

_____

_____

_____

_____

_____

_____

_____

_____

_____

Examine your small stuff and determine what you can live with—without sweating it—and what you really can't stand.

_____

_____

_____

_____

_____

_____

_____

_____

_____

_____

_____

_____

_____

Compliments are unsolicited gifts of appreciation. Accept them with ease, and give them whenever you can.

_____

_____

_____

_____

_____

_____

_____

_____

_____

_____

_____

_____

_____

_____

_____

Keep your well-being intact, and you'll better serve your family, friends, and others around you.

_____

_____

_____

_____

_____

_____

_____

_____

_____

_____

_____

_____

_____

_____

There is a time and place for a little healthy fear. It keeps us safe when applied with a commonsense attitude.

Know your personal boundaries so that you can communicate them to others.

Don't be upset when things don't go as you planned—be pleasantly surprised when things *do* go right!

Doubts let you know when you're out of your comfort zone. When you feel them, use them as an opportunity for growth.

_____

_____

_____

_____

_____

_____

_____

_____

_____

_____

_____

_____

_____

You are human and will make mistakes. Learn from past lessons, and forgive yourself.

_____

_____

_____

_____

_____

_____

_____

_____

_____

_____

_____

_____

_____

Remember that superficial communication creates a shallow existence where little that is true to the heart is shared.

When you have PMS, don't make everything a big deal—
remember that this, too, shall pass.

_____

_____

_____

_____

_____

_____

_____

_____

_____

_____

_____

_____

_____

Don't take on too many nonmandatory tasks. Let others take over, and set limits to avoid being overstressed.

You can learn about yourself from your children. They are great teachers because they reflect so easily what they see.

_____

_____

_____

_____

_____

_____

_____

_____

_____

_____

_____

_____

_____

_____

You will never regret healing a relationship by reaching out to another person and accepting at least half of the responsibility for bad feelings.

_____

_____

_____

_____

_____

_____

_____

_____

_____

_____

_____

_____

Give clothes and other items that you no longer use to those who need and can appreciate them.

_____

_____

_____

_____

_____

_____

_____

_____

_____

_____

_____

_____

_____

Accept that on some issues, two people may never see eye to eye.

_____

_____

_____

_____

_____

_____

_____

_____

_____

_____

_____

_____

_____

_____

It's comforting to know that there are people in your life who have confidence and faith in you.

When you're genuinely happy inside and connected to your spirit, you are lit from within by a radiance that shines from your soul.

_____

_____

_____

_____

_____

_____

_____

_____

_____

_____

_____

_____

Remember that your way is just one of many different ways.

_____

_____

_____

_____

_____

_____

_____

_____

_____

_____

_____

_____

_____

_____

_____

You can often be your own worst judge—focus on all that you do, instead of all that you don't do.

Creating a child is a spiritually enriching experience, not to be feared but to be celebrated.

_____

_____

_____

_____

_____

_____

_____

_____

_____

_____

_____

_____

_____

A quiet mind is your best tool for introspection and an incredible source of creativity.

_____

_____

_____

_____

_____

_____

_____

_____

_____

_____

_____

_____

_____

_____

The things that bother us are fed by our attention to them. Vent your problems once, and move past them.

Evaluate your life often to make sure that you are living it with your own set of values.

_____

_____

_____

_____

_____

_____

_____

_____

_____

_____

_____

_____

_____

Open your emotional suitcase and take a look inside—you may find a few things that you no longer need and can discard.

Just because you have a thought doesn't mean that it's real.
See your negative thoughts as just thoughts, and take them less
seriously.

_____

_____

_____

_____

_____

_____

_____

_____

_____

_____

_____

_____

_____

Incorporate your spirit in all that you do, and you will find fulfillment.

_____

_____

_____

_____

_____

_____

_____

_____

_____

_____

_____

_____

_____

The key to true contentment is to know when your ego is getting the best of you.

You're never too busy to embrace a new person in your life.

_____

_____

_____

_____

_____

_____

_____

_____

_____

_____

_____

_____

_____

Nurture, feed, and cleanse your spirit to stay young and vital.

_____

_____

_____

_____

_____

_____

_____

_____

_____

_____

_____

_____

_____

_____

Your spirit is like a flame inside of you, waiting to be refueled. As you reconnect with your inner spirit, you will heal.

_____

_____

_____

_____

_____

_____

_____

_____

_____

_____

_____

_____

_____

_____

Go ahead and compliment yourself today. When you're feeling good, you'll shine!

_____

_____

_____

_____

_____

_____

_____

_____

_____

_____

_____

_____

_____

Making yourself a garden space is a beautiful way to create a spiritual place to foster peace and serenity. Fill it with personal symbols of your spirit.

_____

_____

_____

_____

_____

_____

_____

_____

_____

_____

_____

_____

_____

The people who challenge or irritate you the most can be your best spiritual teachers. From them, you can learn patience, understanding, and compassion.

Learn to live from the source of your inspiration instead of staying in the rut of your routine. Make spontaneous plans now and then.

Appreciate the fact that most of life is made up of small things and small moments, one right after the other, that play a huge role in a peaceful, happy life.

_____

_____

_____

_____

_____

_____

_____

_____

_____

_____

_____

_____

Reflect upon the people in your life, like your mother, who have sacrificed for you simply because they love you.

The greatest source of unhappiness for us all—single, married, whatever—is wishing that things were different from the way that they are.

_____

_____

_____

_____

_____

_____

_____

_____

_____

_____

_____

_____

_____

Enthusiasm is a key ingredient to success in life. Your genuine enthusiasm can inspire those around you.

_____

_____

_____

_____

_____

_____

_____

_____

_____

_____

_____

_____

_____

You can give yourself permission to say, "Enough is enough."
Don't overload yourself with commitments that you can't keep.

There are no better nurturers than women. Spend time together with your girlfriends, and use your energies to nurture each other.

_____

_____

_____

_____

_____

_____

_____

_____

_____

_____

_____

_____

_____

Find a balance between your own interests and the many things that you do for others. Experience life as an individual, without labeling yourself.

_____

_____

_____

_____

_____

_____

_____

_____

_____

_____

_____

_____

_____

Wake up and see what's going on in your own head. Be aware of your thinking in difficult times and control "thought explosions" that can stress you out.

_____

_____

_____

_____

_____

_____

_____

_____

_____

_____

_____

_____

Live this day for this day only, and feel like the master of your destiny.

_____

_____

_____

_____

_____

_____

_____

_____

_____

_____

_____

_____

_____

_____

Conflict is a part of life. Say what's on your mind with confidence to avoid the stress of unresolved conflicts.

We all need to be hugged, kissed, and touched. Spend time alone with your partner, and get in touch again.

_____

_____

_____

_____

_____

_____

_____

_____

_____

_____

_____

_____

_____

Strive to become the person that others can trust with a secret.

Don't let the scale dictate how you feel or live your life each day. Weigh less often, and live more fully.

One of our true spiritual challenges is to live with conveniences without being overly dependent on them. Just for today, do without a favorite convenience.

_____

_____

_____

_____

_____

_____

_____

_____

_____

_____

_____

_____

_____

Hotheads don't get much accomplished. Being firm and non-reactive will get the responses that you desire.

_____

_____

_____

_____

_____

_____

_____

_____

_____

_____

_____

_____

_____

Don't be afraid to take a break. Time away from your responsibilities is an emotional and spiritual necessity.

_____

_____

_____

_____

_____

_____

_____

_____

_____

_____

_____

_____

_____

_____

There are more stars in the universe than there are grains of sand on the beaches. Remember this when the irritating "small stuff" crops up, and you'll see the wider view of life.

Setting boundaries isn't a negative thing—it simply tells others where you are, what you want, and what you need.

Keeping your composure in the face of others' anger lets you handle conflict from a place of inner strength.

_____

_____

_____

_____

_____

_____

_____

_____

_____

_____

_____

_____

_____

_____

Be aware of the power of prevention—limiting commitments can be the most important aspect of simplifying your life.

Don't brush off friends who want to help you. They truly care about your well-being.

_____

_____

_____

_____

_____

_____

_____

_____

_____

_____

_____

_____

_____

_____

Practice making the irritations in life less of a big deal. You can make the small stuff trivial just as easily as you can blow it out of proportion.

_____

_____

_____

_____

_____

_____

_____

_____

_____

_____

_____

_____

_____

Today, look in the mirror and say, "I am lucky to be born a woman!" Express yourself in your own uniquely feminine way.

_____

_____

_____

_____

_____

_____

_____

_____

_____

_____

_____

_____

_____

_____

_____

Open your eyes to the possibilities in life. When you adopt a positive attitude, you will see possibilities all around you.

_____

_____

_____

_____

_____

_____

_____

_____

_____

_____

_____

_____

_____

_____

Other people and outside circumstances don't make you feel emotions. Your feelings come from you alone.

_____

_____

_____

_____

_____

_____

_____

_____

_____

_____

_____

_____

_____

_____

Don't let your "to do" list consume you! Slow down and be touched by life's simple pleasures and beauty.

Compassion and inner peace go hand in hand. It's almost impossible to be stressed or unhappy when your heart is filled with compassion.

_____

_____

_____

_____

_____

_____

_____

_____

_____

_____

_____

_____

_____

Listen to your feelings—they tell you your current state of mind. If your feelings are low, question your judgment and make allowances for that fact.

_____

_____

_____

_____

_____

_____

_____

_____

_____

_____

_____

_____

You can handle any situation that appears to be an obstacle if you take it one step at a time.

Get used to letting things go instead of clenching your fists and feeling frustrated—you'll feel lighter and more peaceful.

Take charge of your own happiness and emotional well-being, and don't rely on others to fulfill you.

_____

_____

_____

_____

_____

_____

_____

_____

_____

_____

_____

_____

_____

_____

Wake up each day with the intention of seeing life as an incredible adventure.

_____

_____

_____

_____

_____

_____

_____

_____

_____

_____

_____

_____

_____

_____

You can see things more clearly when you're calm and collected. Respond to life; don't just react to it.

_____

_____

_____

_____

_____

_____

_____

_____

_____

_____

_____

_____

_____

_____

What's in the past is in the past, and the future is yet to come. Real life is right here—right now.

_____

_____

_____

_____

_____

_____

_____

_____

_____

_____

_____

_____

_____

_____

A woman with true self-confidence is the most attractive woman in a room.

_____

_____

_____

_____

_____

_____

_____

_____

_____

_____

_____

_____

_____

_____

Live carefree for a few moments each day, like you did when you were a kid. Just get out and play!

Lose your habit of regret—work with what is, rather than wishing that things were different.

Honor your loved ones with your deepest level of understanding.

The key to enjoying life's journey is to be open to the unknown that lies ahead and to accept whatever happens as part of your own personalized life plan.

Making your life better through personal reflection affects everyone around you positively.

_____

_____

_____

_____

_____

_____

_____

_____

_____

_____

_____

_____

_____

_____

Go on a "health binge"—cleanse yourself with fresh fruits, veggies, and juices for three days to detoxify and balance yourself.

_____

_____

_____

_____

_____

_____

_____

_____

_____

_____

_____

_____

If you're blessed with success, give back to the world by supporting a cause that you believe in.

_____

_____

_____

_____

_____

_____

_____

_____

_____

_____

_____

_____

_____

Family life is full of negotiation—it's about bending and blending through better communication.

_____

_____

_____

_____

_____

_____

_____

_____

_____

_____

_____

_____

_____

_____

Don't get caught up in the low moods or emotions of others—
stay centered, and protect your inner flame.

_____

_____

_____

_____

_____

_____

_____

_____

_____

_____

_____

_____

_____

Develop a keen sense of your intuition. It is your "higher self" and gives you the ability to tune in to your own innate wisdom.

_____

_____

_____

_____

_____

_____

_____

_____

_____

_____

_____

_____

_____

Each of your relationships is like a fragile bird in your hand—
don't hold it so tightly that you squeeze the life out of it, nor so
loosely that it flies away. Hold it just right.

Self-doubt is nothing more than a hiccup, a simple reminder that you're pushing yourself—and expanding your potential by doing so.

_____

_____

_____

_____

_____

_____

_____

_____

_____

_____

_____

_____

_____

When you forgive a wrongdoing, you give yourself peace of mind and serenity.

_____

_____

_____

_____

_____

_____

_____

_____

_____

_____

_____

_____

Real joy comes from true feeling. Let it shine and light up the people around you.

Mothers: Empower your daughters with helpful guidance when they ask for it, but don't make their issues your issues.

Live by the standard that if something is in your power to change, you should go ahead and change it.

_____

_____

_____

_____

_____

_____

_____

_____

_____

_____

_____

_____

_____

_____

_____

True beauty happens from the inside out, and will attract others like a magnet.

_____

_____

_____

_____

_____

_____

_____

_____

_____

_____

_____

_____

_____

_____

When you're connected to your own spirit, you know what nourishes you and what doesn't.

_____

_____

_____

_____

_____

_____

_____

_____

_____

_____

_____

_____

Spend time alone with yourself to connect with your spirit and inner beauty.

_____

_____

_____

_____

_____

_____

_____

_____

_____

_____

_____

_____

_____

_____

_____

When you tune in to the present moment and experience it completely, you are truly "in the flow" of creativity, reflection, and inspired thoughts.

_____

_____

_____

_____

_____

_____

_____

_____

_____

_____

_____

_____

Expecting things to always be the way that they were in the past keeps you stuck in the past. Look to the present for a fresh view of the way that things really are.

_____

_____

_____

_____

_____

_____

_____

_____

_____

_____

_____

_____

Use the talents and gifts that the Creator has given you to give back to others through your work.

When you connect with your true self and let it speak, your inspiration and peace of mind soar.

_____

_____

_____

_____

_____

_____

_____

_____

_____

_____

_____

_____

_____

Treat your friends like gold—friendships make your path pleasurable and your experience richer.

You have an abundance of love to give, and your friendships are the place to begin.

_____

_____

_____

_____

_____

_____

_____

_____

_____

_____

_____

_____

_____

_____

_____

Accept the changes in your body as you age, and see your beauty in all of its stages.

_____

_____

_____

_____

_____

_____

_____

_____

_____

_____

_____

_____

_____

The beauty of being human is that we can search for meaning from the inside out and rework our individual tapestry, one thread at a time.

_____

_____

_____

_____

_____

_____

_____

_____

_____

_____

_____

_____

_____

If you knew that you had only one day to live, what would you think about?

_____

_____

_____

_____

_____

_____

_____

_____

_____

_____

_____

_____

_____

Indulge yourself for one day, be it with chocolate cake for break-
fast or by leaving your pajamas on all day. Do what occurs to you
from moment to moment for a change of pace.

Use your day-to-day experiences—including the hassles—to grow, to become more patient, and to become more loving.

_____

_____

_____

_____

_____

_____

_____

_____

_____

_____

_____

_____

_____

There may be many paths in life that lead you to the same destination. Choose the ones with doors that open when you knock. These are the paths of least resistance.

_____

_____

_____

_____

_____

_____

_____

_____

_____

_____

_____

_____

_____

_____

If you find yourself putting out great efforts in life without achieving your desired results, it's a sign for you to move on in a different direction.

Compassion grows with practice. Spend a little time each day reflecting on how you can be of service—the rest will take care of itself.

_____

_____

_____

_____

_____

_____

_____

_____

_____

_____

_____

_____

_____

Don't contemplate the future; don't dwell on the past—challenges are far less overwhelming if you solve them in the moment with baby steps.

_____

_____

_____

_____

_____

_____

_____

_____

_____

_____

_____

_____

_____

Life gives you all of what you need and some of what you ask for.
Every event has purpose and meaning.

_____

_____

_____

_____

_____

_____

_____

_____

_____

_____

_____

_____

_____

_____